Blue Muse

ELBA SOLER

LitPrime Solutions
21250 Hawthorne Blvd
Suite 500, Torrance, CA 90503
www.litprime.com
Phone: 1 (209) 788-3500

© 2021 Elba Soler. All rights reserved.

No part of this book may be reproduced, stored in a retrieval system, or transmitted by any means without the written permission of the author.

Published by LitPrime Solutions   04/01/2021

ISBN: 978-1-953397-85-0(sc)
ISBN: 978-1-953397-86-7(hc)
ISBN: 978-1-953397-87-4(e)

Any people depicted in stock imagery provided by iStock are models, and such images are being used for illustrative purposes only.

Certain stock imagery © iStock.

Because of the dynamic nature of the Internet, any web addresses or links contained in this book may have changed since publication and may no longer be valid. The views expressed in this work are solely those of the author and do not necessarily reflect the views of the publisher, and the publisher hereby disclaims any responsibility for them.

Contents

I Was Born v
In Retrospect vii

Acrostic (Mine) 1
Alone I Cry 3
Anguish 5
Are You The One? 7
As You Cross The Bridge 9
Ashes 13
Be Stingy 15
Betrayed 17
Bite Your Tongue 21
But Time. 25
Happy Together 29
I Gave You My Heart 31
I Heard 35
I Still See You 37
I Weep Thru My Pen 39
I'm Not Alone 41
In My Heart 45
Just Like A Flower 47
Leaves 49
Like The Dew 51
Mourning The Morn 53
My Husband 55
Pain, Pain Go Away 57
Silver Threads 59
Since You've Been Gone 61

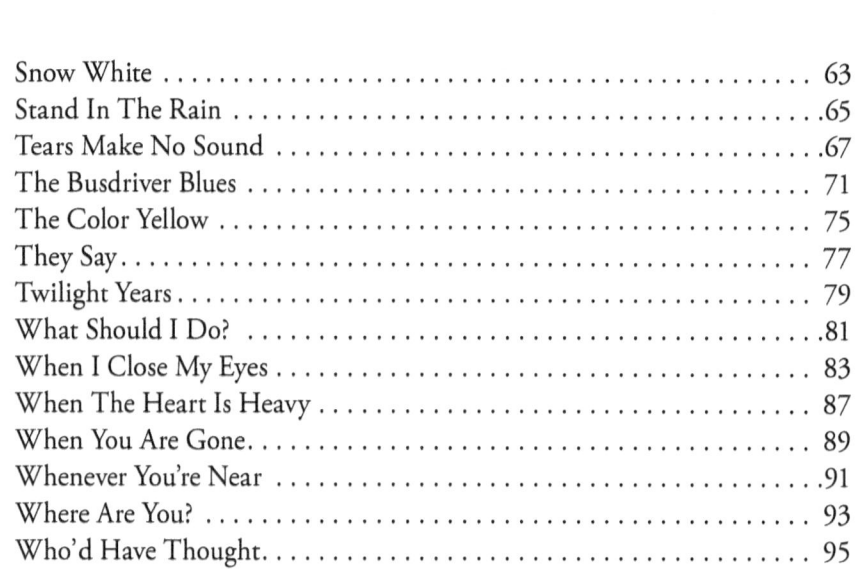

Snow White	63
Stand In The Rain	65
Tears Make No Sound	67
The Busdriver Blues	71
The Color Yellow	75
They Say	77
Twilight Years	79
What Should I Do?	81
When I Close My Eyes	83
When The Heart Is Heavy	87
When You Are Gone	89
Whenever You're Near	91
Where Are You?	93
Who'd Have Thought	95

I Was Born

I was born in the enchanted island of Puerto Rico, USA, to a military dad. My parents were divorced when I was nine. I was uprooted and tossed about between them and my grandmother. I went to nine different schools, which made it very difficult to "grow" relationships. During my growing years I felt like a flower that was cut and not allowed to bloom; dehydrated and uprooted, neglected and forgotten, deprived of care and affection... Well, not knowing how to express myself or who to turn to, I poured out my heart into my poetry. This poem is a reflection of how I felt. Read on and feel...

In Retrospect

It was 1963, the year President Kennedy was killed. I was fifteen, living with my grandmother, attending an all girl Catholic school, when my friend invited me to her sweet sixteen birthday party. Mamá, as I called my grandmother, said: "No, you can't go, I don't know those people." So my friend's parents had to come in person to meet her and invite me, assuring her that they would personally pick me up and drive me back, and look after me as if I was one of their daughters.

At the party I met my friend's older brother, who introduced me to his co-worker friends, Johnny and Alberto. Both were vying for my attention, but Alberto insisted on riding home with me. He called me the next day, and the next, and the next. Mamá was getting upset. Then, he asked to speak to her and asked her if he could visit me. Surprisingly, she agreed.

The first time Alberto came, he brought a dozen pink roses. While I was putting them in a vase, Mamá motioned him to sit at one end of the sofa, and then she sat in the middle of it, so I had to sit at the other end!

The next time, Alberto didn't bring me roses. Instead, he brought a box of chocolates and handed them to Mamá. But she again sat in the middle of the sofa. Realizing that she wasn't going to budge from that, he asked her if he could take me out to the Art Museum next time. Again, surprisingly, she agreed!

But when Alberto came, the surprised one was he. For Mamá had arranged for both my aunt and my uncle to chaperone us.

That was the first and last time we went out. Alberto's parting comment was that it was easier to rob an armored Brink's truck than to get to first base with me. . . Whatever that meant.

Elba Soler
January 17, 2009.

Acrostic (Mine)

Mine I want you to be;
Inflamed with love I have been; (Indeed, love has stricken me!)
Great is the passion that burns
Deep, deep, inside of me.
As the air that you breathe,
Life without it, can't be,
Intrinsically, my darling,
Air you are to me!

Elba Soler

Alone I Cry

As much as I try,
I can't forget you.
Alone I cry,
Because you
Have poisoned my life
With a deep love wound.
But what do you care…
If my bosom weeps?
…If my heart bleeds?
If you've never felt
A grief so deep.
I will carry the burden
And drown my bitter sorrow
For a love that cannot be.

Elba Soler

Anguish

Anguish,
Watching the flame of life extinguish,
Feeling abandoned,
Thirsting for a tender touch,
Hungry for a bit of love…
I don't want to
Lower myself
And ask, and beg,
And tell you
I can't go on like this;
From my lonesome sadness,
The tree of life wilting,
Watching the dead leaves
Of my youth
Fall to my feet…

Elba Soler

Are You The One?

My beloved,
Are you The one
I've been waiting for?
The one to fulfill my dreams?
Hopes, Expectations;
Will all come to fruition… ?
Because All
Revolves around you.
Love me like I love you.
End all anxiety.
You are the one I've waited for.

Elba Soler

As You Cross The Bridge

That transcends
From a single life
To another of commitment,
Remember the old proverb:
"It is best to give
Than to receive."
Soon you will take the step
That will tie your destiny
Of giving yourself
Fully to the one you love.
"Two will come together
To become one,"
To fill the void
We all have.
As it states in the Bible,
God said:
"It is not good
For man to be alone."
As two half-full cups,
It is necessary to pour one

Into the other,
So both will be fulfilled.
Give it all,
So joy can be achieved.
Life is full of hues;
Vivid colors, and gray ones too.
They compliment each other,
And highlight the other.
You will have highs,
And you will have lows.
But if both share the same feeling,
And only one thought:
To make the other happy,
When one is down,
Extend out your hand
To bring up your partner.
And when you see the other smile,
You'll both end up smiling!

Elba Soler

Ashes

You came into my life
Like a tornado,
Bearing strife,
Tearing down
Everything along your path.
Like a hurricane
Whose time has passed,
You moved on,
Notwithstanding pain
And desolation.
And if you attempt
To tempt me,
Stirring up the ruins
That you yourself
Left behind,
Only ashes will you find
Of that burning fire
That consumed all desire.

Elba Soler
2/1/2010

Be Stingy

Be stingy with your complaints,
But be generous with your compliments.
They say I'm so stingy,
I even use few words.
But I'd rather just listen,
Than impose my views on them.
If I can't say something positive,
I'd rather not make any comment.

I have found that when my mouth is open,
I can't hear what others have spoken.
Maybe that's today's problem;
People are too busy talking,
Sharing their opinions with "them",
Even if they don't edify,
But rather hurt, disparage and smother.
So I'll be stingy, for the moment,
With my complaints and comments,
So as not to hurt others.

Elba Soler
11/28/2017
Valdosta, GA

Betrayed

Oh! How it hurts to be betrayed…
There are things
That even time can't erase;
I will continue to sing,
Enjoy life, love and dance,
But if by chance
I remember your name,
Or your kiss,
I wipe my lips,
And wash my face,
Still, There remains
An indelible trace….
What you thought
Was love forevermore
Turned out to be a fling.
Your trust is lost,
You feel crushed…
Though your tears
You may swallow,
So as not to wallow
In your worst fears,

In your anguish you choke
When you evoke
The promise of love
That the wind blew away…
It's futile to pretend,
The unforeseen end
Has found its way…
There's nothing more
To look for
In tomorrow.
I lie awake…
Who'd have said
That at my age
I'd make a fool of myself.
As the old sage
Says: there's no bigger fool
And none so blind
Than he who will not see…
I closed my eyes
And you were all I could see.

Elba Soler ©

Bite Your Tongue

Learn to bite your tongue
Before your bite the hand
That feeds you,
Or before long
You may have to lick that hand
With your tail between your legs.
Right where you stand
You have a roof over your head.
Any regrets?
Step out in the cold,
Under the pouring rain,
Feel my pain.
Maybe then you'll appreciate
What you've gained
And hold back your disdain.
Which is better?
Anger, hunger or hurt?
Anger begets anger,
Hurt begets hurt.

So watch your words.
They're like bullets
That penetrate
Deep into the soul.
I've been told
When Humpty-Dumpty falls
Off the wall,
The broken pieces won't hold.
So watch your words.
Theyr'e like a double sword
That cuts both ways.
Are you dismayed?
You thought I could be swayed
With double talk
After your verbal assault?
Think again...

Elba Soler

But Time

But is the bud
Of hopelessness.
But is getting stuck
In the mud;
You can spin your wheels around,
But only a positive wedge
Will get you out of the rut.
Negativity is a malignancy;
Stop it, or it will stop you.
Doubt is a cloud…
But there is no clout in doubt.
Failure to believe,
Breeds failure to try;
Failure to try is failure.
Attitude affects our actions;
Belief determines behavior;
Together they spell BIG things.
Active faith is alive.
Fail to act, and you die.
Therefore, redeem the time.
Everyone has been given time.
What counts
Is what you do with it…

You will be called
To give account.
Time is no respecter of persons.
Eat healthy, exercise, stay fit…
But time will not stay still
The world turns, the clock turns,
And any way you turn,
When it's your turn,
Time will run out in the end.
Today is a gift;
That's why it's called: the present.
So don't waste it.
Wasting is a sin.
Call it whatever you want,
But sin is still sin.
Time is a relative means
By which we measure
The passing of events;
What we've done with it
Is our treasure!

Elba Soler

Happy Together

They are envious
To see us
Together,
As we walk down the street
Happily holding hands;
And they want to sever
Our love
From its roots,
A love
They never
Could have.
Without your kisses
I die of thirst,
And you without mine
Could not last.
We love each other,
What are we to do...
If life wanted to
Brings us together?

Elba Soler
12/29/2015?
Valdosta, GA

I Gave You My Heart

How do you break apart
When two have become one?
The song says breaking up is hard to do…
But I guess it's for the best…
And I really wish you the best.
I knew from the start
That it wouldn't last,
Given the difference in age,
But I cherish every moment I had with you…
Anyway, I'm returning your gifts
So you don't feel that "you're out."
I never wanted anything from you,
But to be with you.
I'm grateful for the good moments we had.
All I want from you now
Is to give me back my heart,

Which I gave to you bit by bit
With every kiss…
Can you do that?
I thought you might want to see
The fallen tree
In front of my house,
So here's a photo…
I feel like that tree:
Fallen and cut into pieces,
Then hauled away to the dumpster
Like unwanted trash…
Such is life…
May you have a blessed life…

Love always,
Elba

I Heard

I heard you've been bad,
And that makes me sad.
I used to be glad;
I could always brag:
My grandkids are the greatest;
Well mannered
And well behaved…
You were always the best.
So I hope it's just a phase
That will soon pass,
So I can shout out loud:
You make me so proud!
I heard you did good
In school,
And I think that's cool.
And for what it's worth
Just remember:
You're doing it for yourself!

Elba R. Soler

I Still See You

I still see you
Dressed in white,
In a cloud of lace,
Coming down the isle ...
Walking at your own pace
To meet me at the altar...

Destiny tried
To set us apart;
But Providence
Brought us together,
Because she knew our hearts.

Now it's sealed in a pact;
We'll spend our lives together,
Walking along the same path...
Until one of us departs.

Elba Soler

I Weep Thru My Pen

Youth, divine treasure,
Gone forever,
Never to return,
With the elusive dream
Of yesterday,
Washed away
By the rain.
Deflowered
And withered rose
Of love,
All illusion
Killed by pain;
Sometimes
When I grief
The tears won't flow;
Other times
I weep thru my pen…

Elba Soler
8/3/2012?
Valdosta, GA

I'm Not Alone

I went to the shore
By the sea
And the waves said to me
You no longer loved me;
And I responded:
I don't know
Why my love is so.
Is there no hope?
Then I heard
A voice from above:
"There's no need
To weep;
My love for you is so deep,
Your tears I can't bear to see."
Then heaven was moved
To compassion
And tears from above
Came down and touched
My aching soul.
I felt the soft wind

Caressing my skin,
Playing with my hair,
And all my cares
Vanished into thin air.
I saw the Son show
His love
Thru His warm glow.
I saw the Light
And my plight
Departed;
As the clouds parted
It no longer mattered
That you were gone,
For now I know
I'm not alone!

Elba Soler

In My Heart

Love cannot be demanded;
It must be freely given.
In my heart
You'll always be mine;
No one can love you
The way I have…
You don't know
What it feels like
When someone you love
Doesn't love you back.
I know that in the end
You will regret
Having parted
And will want
To come back.
I hope by then
You'll realize…
You gambled with the prize
And you lost…
I may have found
Another love!

Elba Soler
10/24/2010
Valdosta, GA

Just Like A Flower

A gardener
Plants a flower,
Then he goes away.
Another one comes along,
Loving and tender
To cultivate;
To whom does it belong?

Love is like a flower:
It takes sunshine
And showers.
If there's no joy,
If there's no peace,;
If only thorns
We seem to reap,
From the storm of our soul
A lightning flashes;
A smile, though so weak.

Just like a flower,
Life is very brief;
By outward laughter
Be not deceived;
While deep down we weep,
We wither without love,
And we die out of grief.

Elba Soler
4/7/2005?

Leaves

Because I don't rake the leaves
They call me slovenly;
But I like to see the leaves;
They keep me company.
I watch them stir,
And move and tremble
As if tickled by the breeze;
And twirl and tumble,
Swinging in the wind,
Until they kiss the ground beneath
At the foot of the tree.

Elba R. Soler

Like The Dew

Like the dew
In the morning
Touches the grass
When it's wilting,
So is man
In his mourning;
God's loving spirit
Touches his heart
And even in his grief
He finds relief.

Elba Soler

Mourning The Morn

As the evening hangs
The shadows are reborn,
In the still of the dark
I hear a whine spark
A sad song of love,
A woe of mourn,
A deep sorrow,
A bittersweet song
That weeps all night long
For the return of the morn.

Elba Soler

My Husband

My Husband,
My lover,
My confidant,
My soul brother,
My companion,
My life-partner,
My best friend.

Elba R. Soler

Gimpy, but not wimpy! (His own words)
*His favorite quotes from the JC Creed: *

THE JAYCEE CREED

We believe:
* That faith in God gives meaning and purpose to human life;
* That the brotherhood of man transcends the sovereignty of nations;
  - That economic justice can best be won by free men through free enterprise;
  - That government should be of laws rather than of men;
  - *That earth's great treasure lies in human personality; and
  - *That service to humanity is the best work of life.

Pain, Pain Go Away

I was standing under a dark cloud
And I said out loud:
Rain, rain, go away;
Come back some other day…
Then I became aware
There were no raindrops in my hair;
But tears rolling down my face.
Oh! If only the pain
Would go away…
If I hurt my back
I could wear a brace;
If I hurt my leg
I could walk with a cane;
If I broke my arm
I could wear a cast…
But what to do
When you're torn apart
With a broken heart?

Elba Soler

Silver Threads

When the silver threads
Begin to show,
Like the moon
Reflected
On the blue lagoon,
I will cry like a baby
Upon awakening,
For then I'll know
My youth is gone,
And I'll cry alone…

Elba R. Soler

Since You've Been Gone

For a long time now,
I long to hear your voice
And feel your love…
I no longer know
What it is to live,
What it is to sing,
When you're not around.
Every sound
I perceive
Makes me think,
Makes me feel
So empty inside…
And I sigh,
'Cause I can't conceive
Life…
Without you.
Gone is the flower
You took with your absence;
The nights are cold,
The sun shine's not gold…
Since you've been gone
Only tears fill my soul.

Elba Soler

Snow White

When October comes around,
I like to see the snow-white covered ground;
Not the cold snow of the North,
Though awesome to look at
When I'm inside looking out,
But the cotton covered ground
Of the warm, beautiful South!

Elba Soler
10/22/2018
Valdosta, GA

Stand In The Rain

Whenever I would read poems
I thought with disdain:
Go stand in the rain
So the showers can clear your head.
I guess I had never felt
The wonder love can bring;
Like the vibration
When bells ring;
Sheer exhilaration
At the touch of your skin;
Brimming excitement
In expectation
At the sight of you…
Then along came you;
Now I need to stand in the rain.

Elba R. Soler
12/18/2011?
Valdosta, GA

Tears Make No Sound

Tears make no sound
As they fall,
But my heart
Is bleeding to death.
You can't understand
My pain at all,
But it hurts
With every breath.

Tears make no sound
As they roll down;
But my heart
Is dying in silence.
Can't you understand
My sorrow?
For me there's no tomorrow
In your absence.

Don't think
Because I sing,
That my heart is happy
And content;
I sing from my soul
To console
Myself.

Deep down,
I weep disconsolate,
I feel isolate,
Alone and desperate,
And full of discontent.

Oh! Youth, divine treasure,
Gone forever,
Never to return;
My grief has no measure;
I find no consolation,
Only thorns my feet tread,
I swallow
My sorrow,
So I laugh instead.

Elba Soler
Valdosta, GA
5/25/2005

The Busdriver Blues

When you are gone
Who will take your place?
I just want you to be safe,
Because you alone
Are so very special.
I know you don't care
About how I feel,
You have a heart of steel,
As I did before
I knew my Lord.
You cause me grief
Whenever I see
You're courting danger.
I should feel anger,
Because even though
In my mind
I know
It's no fault of mine

What happens to you,
Just with the thought
Some harm could befall you,
My heart feels the burden
Of deep sorrow.
Don't you want to know
The promise of tomorrow?
Don't throw your life away;
Don't just live for the moment,
The thrill of today
Will be become your sorrow. . .
When you look back with regret
At what could have been,
Should have been,
But is not… yet.

Elba Soler – bus 17

The Color Yellow

Ms. Katherine Hepburn,
I beg to disagree.
You said no one looks good in yellow,
But from what I can see,
I find that color so mellow.
Next to blue and green
It's so cool, like mint.
Next to red and orange
It's so hot, I can feel it singe;
It makes my blood curdle.
Put it next to purple,
It surmounts the royal hurdle.
Pair it with black,
It's cheerful, not sad.
So tell me, Ms. Katherine,
Why you think yellow is so bad?

Elba R. Soler

They Say

I'm living a fantasy;
Love is a thing
Of which only fools sing,
There can't be love
Between fall and spring.
But I say
No one can know
What our hearts feel.
Deep down inside
At the thought of you
I sigh…
You may have been sly,
You may have told me lies…
But your words
Were like sunshine,
Manna from the sky…
Bringing light
Into my dark life…
Oh, how I miss you!
… Your warm and tender touch…
You may not know this:
But I love you so much…!

Elba Soler ©

Twilight Years

Silver threads
Weave the tapestry on my head.
Deep furrow lines
Design
The character of my face.
My walk,
Once swift,
Has now slowed
To a turtle's pace. ...
My back,
Once tall and erect,
Hunches over
With the burden
Of time's weight.
Though it appears
The fire has gone out,
Deep down
In my soul,
The candle still burns
For the love
Of my twilight years,
That I hold
So dear.

Elba Soler

What Should I Do?

Where can I go?
Will somebody tell me,
For I do not know…?
Why must I live,
If nobody wants me,
If nobody loves
This wandering soul;
If I am to live
And die all alone?
Do you know the answer?
Then tell me, oh Lord!
I'm so desperate…
Have mercy, have mercy
On my poor soul!
Don't abandon me,
Now that life's so dull;
Now that all around me
Has no meaning at all;
Now that my love
Has left me,
Now that my love is gone…
What Should I Do?
Where can I go?
Tell me, oh Lord, tell me,
For I do not know!

Elba Soler
Rio Piedras, P.R.
7/8/1967

When I Close My Eyes

When I close my eyes
I see you as yesterday.
With its pitter-patter,
In a quiet chatter,
I hear the rain say:
Oh! What does it matter?
Now he's gone away;
Come, I whisper,
I need you to listen;
If you don't come today,
Tomorrow
Will be too late.
I'm so disconsolate;
I will drown in my sorrow;
Have pity on my pain.
I am wearied
With so much weeping…
And speaking
To myself
Of things past,
I feel my heart,
Come to a halt,

As I listen with regret.
It's not your fault,
I hear myself say,
I drove you away...
My love was so great,
It must have felt
Like a smother.
You had to be free
To play
And flutter.

Just like a flower,
Life is very brief;
By outward laughter
Be not deceived;
While deep down we weep,
We wither without love
And we die out of grief.

Elba Soler
Valdosta, GA
8/3/2003

When The Heart Is Heavy

When the clouds are too heavy
The rain begins to fall;
When the heart is too heavy
The teardrops roll…
Don't waste your words
On who won't listen;
Don't send messages
To who won't respond;
Don't waste your time
On who doesn't deserve you.
Do people change with time,
Or does time make them show
Who they really are?
The past can not be erased,
Deleted, edited or defaced;
Only your attitude
Can be changed.
So accept what's done,
Move on with your life;
Look forward
And not behind.
Time marches on.

When You Are Gone

When you are gone
I'll be surrounded by shadows.
When you are gone
I'll be alone
With my sorrow.
I will silently evoke
Those tender moments
Of love
In the vague darkness
Of my quiet room,
Where one afternoon
I felt your warm caress.
My arms will long for you,
My lips will search for yours;
I will breathe in the air
And remember our love affair,
And that scent of lavender,
And your soft hair…
When you are gone
I'll be so alone
With my despair.

Elba Soler
5/25/2005
Valdosta, GA

Whenever You're Near

My heart beats wildly
Whenever you're near
But I can't let you know
Just how I feel. . .
Because I fear
A possible rejection…
And that, my dear,
Would mean dejection.

Where Are You?

Where are you, my love?
I can't feel your heartbeat;
My grief is so deep
I can't even weep.
I want to cry out
But the tears choke up
In my throat;
The well has dried out.
I loved you
More than my life,
But on a cold morning
You gave me the cold shoulder,
Tossed me aside
Like a broken toy…
Now there's no more joy
In my life;
My heart is mourning
The loss of your love…

Elba Soler ©

Who'd Have Thought

Who'd have thought
That at this stage in my life,
When most everything is forgotten,
That I would finally find
Who would unite to my destiny
And give me his company.

Holding hands
We venture thru the world;
Life goes on…
While we rest,
We watch the sundown,
Whispering: "I love you!"

Hearing his snoring,
Like a cat's purring,
A pleasant feeling takes over,
As sleep hovers,
In a peaceful hold,
In his warm embrace, I doze off.

I wake up yawning;
I see his white hair;
I touch his forehead
To feel his warmth,
And his chest palpitates...
And I thank God!

Elba Soler
Valdosta, GA 2020

www.ingramcontent.com/pod-product-compliance
Lightning Source LLC
Chambersburg PA
CBHW021429070526
44577CB00001B/127